THE SIT STILL GAME

W9-BEW-196

To my mother, Frances Shapiro —LS

To Sachiko Kimura —HT

It's Time to
Sit Still in Your Own Chair

a transition times book

Lawrence E. Shapiro, Ph.D.
Illustrated by **Hideko Takahashi**

Instant Help Books

Talia was a very active little girl.

**She loved to run and jump
and tumble and spin.**

She didn't like to sit still.

At dinner, Talia ate a few bites, then stood on her chair and danced.

At church on Sunday, Talia
squirmed and kicked the seat
in front of her.

At preschool, Talia's classmates sat quietly and colored.

But Talia wouldn't sit still like the other kids.

"It's time to sit still in your own chair," said Talia's teacher.

One evening, Talia was at a fancy restaurant with her parents for Grammy's birthday.

The restaurant was loud
and busy, and the grown-ups
were having fun.

Talia was done eating before the grown-ups had even started!

Talia stood up and danced on her chair. Mommy told her to sit down like a big kid.

Talia snuck under the table to tickle Daddy's legs.

Daddy lifted Talia up and said,
"You're a big girl now. It's time
to sit in your own chair."

Talia cried. Sitting still in her chair was no fun at all.

The next night at the dinner table,
Talia had a new place mat with
happy faces and a box of crayons.

THE SIT STILL GAME

Mommy said, "When you
sit still in your chair, you can
color in a happy face."

"If you are not sitting in your chair, I will count 1 2 3. Then, if you sit quietly, you can color in a happy face."

Daddy said, "If you color in all four of the happy faces, you will get special stickers after dinner."

Talia sat in her chair and ate her applesauce. Mommy told her she could color in a happy face.

THE SIT STILL GAME

Talia drank some of her milk.
Daddy told her she could color
in a happy face.

Talia sat and told Mommy and Daddy about her day. Then she asked, "May I color in a happy face now?" Mommy said, "Yes."

By the end of dinner, Talia had colored in all four happy faces.

Talia got two special stickers
and two special hugs.

Advice for Parents

Dear Parents,

Most children are very active when they first learn to walk, toddle, and then run. Their new mobility opens up an exciting world for exploration, and many children have a hard time sitting still for more than a few minutes at a time.

But by the time children are three years old, they should be able to sit in a chair for fifteen minutes or more. Certainly they should be able to sit through dinner and do seat-work with other children at preschool. If your child can't sit in his seat by the age of three for at least fifteen minutes, this storybook and **The Sit Still Game** program it describes might do the trick.

Teaching your child to sit in his chair is just one aspect of self-control that your child will have to learn. As he grows, there will be more and more demands on him to control his behavior as well as his emotions.

Patience is truly a virtue, not only for the sake of parents who get tired of constantly reminding their children to behave, but also for children themselves. In fact, studies tell us that children who have good self-control consistently achieve more in school and cope better with the inevitable challenges of growing up. Impulsive children are more likely to have serious behavior problems as they grow older. **The Sit Still Game** can help your young child learn to follow important household and school rules. When it is used consistently, you will start to see your child become much more cooperative and easygoing.

Here are some other things you can try, too:

- **When sitting at the table, in the car, or even in the living room, include your child in the conversation so that he feels important.**
- **Praise him frequently when he sits quietly and does what you want.**

- **If you need him to sit longer than he is used to, such as when waiting at a doctor's office or going on a long car ride, make sure that he has something to draw on or play with.**
- **Avoid too much time in front of the television. This might keep your little one still, but it won't teach him self-control. Studies suggest that too much TV will make some children even more inattentive.**

You can print out your own copy of **The Sit Still Game** at our website: www.TransitionTimesBooks.com. You will also find information about different ways to use a reward program and what to do if it doesn't quite work the way you expected. There are also some fun ideas to help you teach your active child more self-control. These include games, relaxation exercises, and positive discipline tips.

As you probably know, there are some children who are slower to develop self-control than others. These children are simply born with a lot of energy and a high need for activity. Parents might be doing everything just right, and still these children can't stay in their seat.

An estimated 4 to 6% of children have some form of attention-deficit / hyperactivity disorder or other neurological problem, making it very hard for them to sit still and concentrate. The good news is that 75% of children with ADHD will outgrow this problem. The bad news is that this might not happen until they are young adults.

If you think that your child is overactive, and he does not respond to a positive behavior program such as the one suggested in this book, then you should talk to your pediatrician and consider consulting a psychologist or learning specialist. If your child is in preschool, his teacher will be a good person to help you develop age-appropriate expectations.

There are many ways to help overactive children, including, but certainly not limited to, medication. Gathering all the information you can and making proactive choices will always be the right course.

Good luck!
Lawrence Shapiro, Ph.D.

The **transition times** series is designed to help parents understand the importance of addressing developmental issues at the right time and in the right way. Each book addresses a specific transition in the lives of children, when they often need a gentle nudge forward on the road to responsibility and independence. The books provide parents with a way to talk to their children that will hold their interest and make facing life's challenges seem less overwhelming. The books also help parents understand age-appropriate expectations, and give them a simple and clear context to set realistic limits. Reading the books to children will make bumpy transition times just a little bit smoother.

Publisher's Note

This publication is sold with the understanding that the publisher is not engaged in render-
ing psychological or other professional services. If expert assistance or counseling is needed,
the services of a competent professional should be sought.

An Instant Help Book

Distributed in Canada by Raincoast Books

Text copyright © 2008 by Lawrence Shapiro, Ph.D.
New Harbinger Publications, Inc.
5674 Shattuck Avenue
Oakland, CA 94609
www.newharbinger.com

Illustrations by Hideko Takahashi
Cover and text design by Amy Shoup
Acquired by Tesilya Hanauer
The illustrations were done in acrylic paint on multimedia paper.
This book was typeset in Souvenir BT.

Library of Congress Cataloging-in-Publication Data
Shapiro, Lawrence E.
  It's time to sit in your own chair : a transition time book / Lawrence E. Shapiro.
     p. cm. -- (Transition times)
  ISBN-13: 978-1-57224-588-4 (hardcover : alk. paper)
  ISBN-10: 1-57224-588-3 (hardcover : alk. paper) 1. Child psychology. 2. Attachment
behavior in children. 3. Child rearing. I. Title.
  BF723.A75S53 2008
  649'.6--dc22

                                        2008029597

All Rights Reserved
Printed in Thailand

10   09   08

10   9   8   7   6   5   4   3   2   1

First printing

Northport-East Northport Public Library

To view your patron record from a computer, click on the Library's homepage: **www.nenpl.org**

You may:
- request an item be placed on hold
- renew an item that is overdue
- view titles and due dates checked out on your card
- view your own outstanding fines

151 Laurel Avenue
Northport, NY 11768
631-261-6930